THE EUGÉNIE ROCHEROLLE SERIES

Intermediate Piano Solo

New Orleans Sketches

6 Original Piano Solos by Eugénie Rocherolle

To all the great New Orleans musicians who made the good times roll.

To access audio visit:
www.halleonard.com/mylibrary

Enter Code
1637-2643-2456-9015

ISBN 978-1-4950-0749-1

7777 W. BLUEMOUND RD. P.O. BOX 13819 MILWAUKEE, WI 53213

In Australia Contact:
Hal Leonard Australia Pty. Ltd.
4 Lentara Court
Cheltenham, Victoria, 3192 Australia
Email: ausadmin@halleonard.com.au

Visit Hal Leonard Online at
www.halleonard.com

FROM THE COMPOSER

I feel fortunate to have been born and raised in the colorful and carefree city of New Orleans where no excuse is ever needed for a party! What better way to communicate this fun-loving atmosphere than through its music. No event, big or small, can be without it—from the strutting marching bands in the carnival parades to a few jazz musicians on a street corner drawing a small crowd. Its music is such an important part of the fabric of the city, adding to every festivity and celebration and providing year-round entertainment in the legendary French Quarter.

It was during my formative years that I absorbed the sounds of Dixieland jazz, spirituals, gospel hymns, and "rhythm & blues." Playing popular music by ear at a young age and learning to coordinate boogie patterns contributed to the harmonic and rhythmic vocabulary that I drew upon in later years. Though I am ever grateful for my lifelong exposure to classical music, there is something about the indigenous music of New Orleans that will always speak to me in a very special way.

Eugénie

Eugénie Rocherolle
February 2015

CONTENTS

4   Big Easy Blues

7   Bourbon Street Beat

10   Carnival Capers

13   Jivin' in Jackson Square

16   Masquerade!

20   Rex Parade

BIG EASY BLUES

By EUGÉNIE ROCHEROLLE

*Pedal optional until last two measures.

BOURBON STREET BEAT

By EUGÉNIE ROCHEROLLE

CARNIVAL CAPERS

By EUGÉNIE ROCHEROLLE

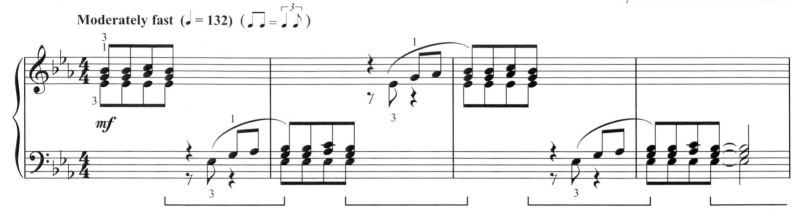

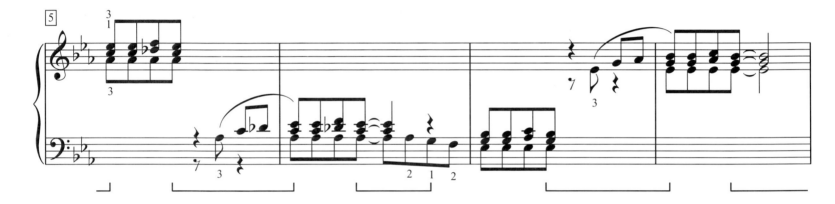

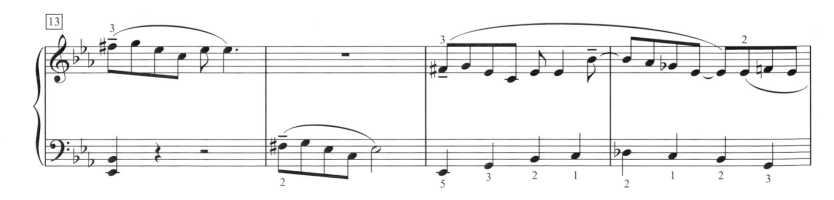

JIVIN' IN JACKSON SQUARE

By EUGÉNIE ROCHEROLLE

MASQUERADE!

By EUGÉNIE ROCHEROLLE

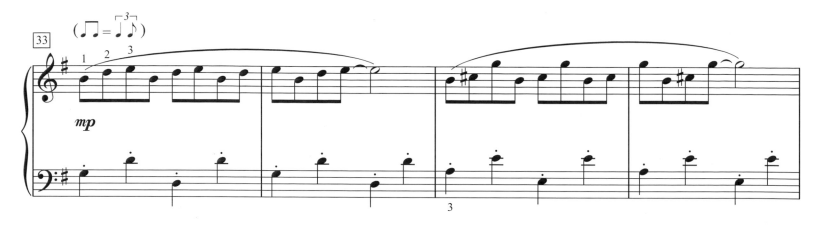

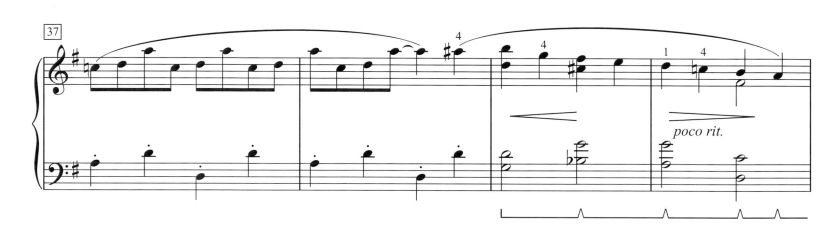

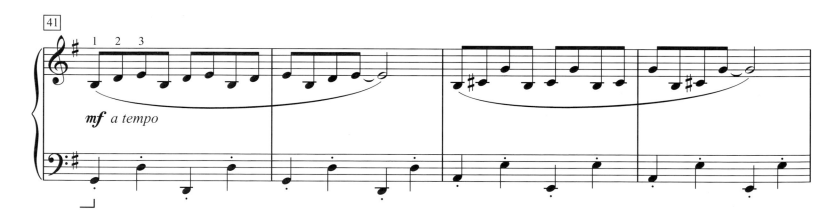

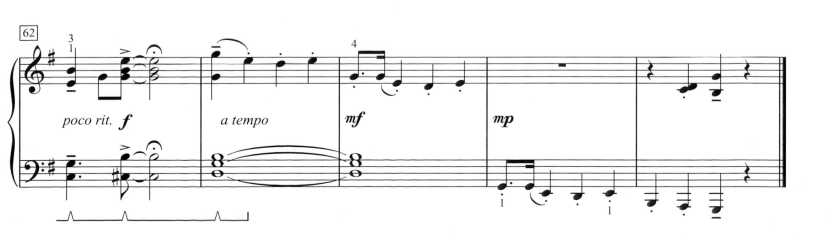

REX PARADE

By EUGÉNIE ROCHEROLLE

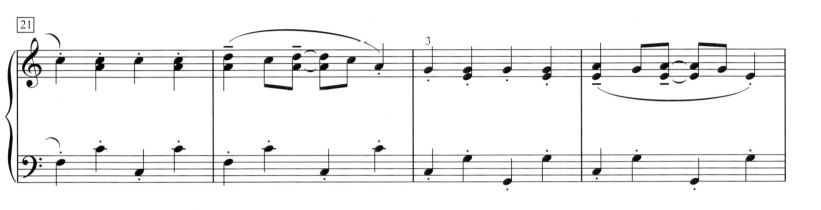

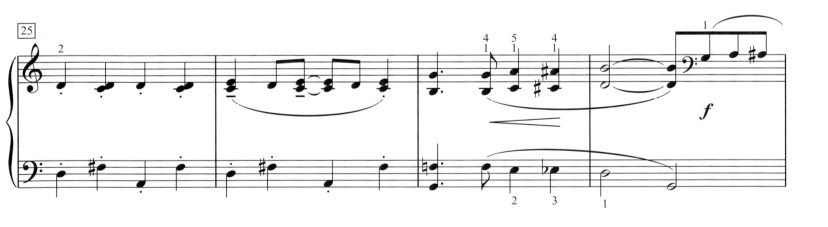

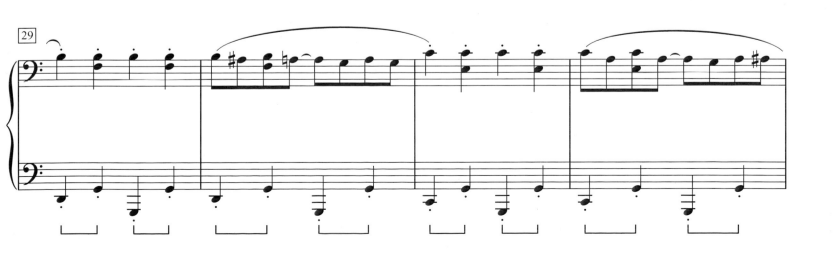

THE EUGÉNIE ROCHEROLLE SERIES

Offering both original compositions and popular arrangements, these stunning collections are ideal for intermediate-level pianists! Many include audio tracks performed by Ms. Rocherolle.

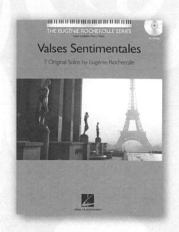

Candlelight Christmas
Eight traditional carols: Away in a Manger • Coventry Carol • Joseph Dearest, Joseph Mine • O Holy Night (duet) • O Little Town of Bethlehem • Silent Night • The Sleep of the Infant Jesus • What Child Is This?
00311808..$14.99

Christmas Together
Six piano duet arrangements: Blue Christmas • The Christmas Song (Chestnuts Roasting on an Open Fire) • Rudolph the Red-Nosed Reindeer • Santa Baby • Up on the Housetop • We Wish You a Merry Christmas.
00102838 ....$14.99

Classic Jazz Standards
Ten beloved tunes: Blue Skies • Georgia on My Mind • Isn't It Romantic? • Lazy River • The Nearness of You • On the Sunny Side of the Street • Stardust • Stormy Weather • and more.
00311424..$12.99

Continental Suite
Six original piano solos: Belgian Lace • In Old Vienna • La Piazza • Les Avenues De Paris • Oktoberfest • Rondo Capichio.
00312111..$12.99

Fantasia del Tango
Six original piano solos (and a bonus piano duet!): Bailando Conmigo • Debajo las Estrellas • Ojos de Coqueta • Promesa de Amor • Suenos de Ti • Suspiros • Tango Caprichoso.
00199978 ....$12.99

George Gershwin – Three Preludes
Accessible for intermediate-level pianists: Allegro ben ritmato e deciso • Andante con moto e poco rubato • Agitato.
00111939 ....$10.99

It's Me, O Lord
Nine traditional spirituals: Deep River • It's Me, O Lord • Nobody Knows De Trouble I See • Swing Low, Sweet Chariot • and more.
00311368..$12.99

Mancini Classics
Songs: Baby Elephant Walk • Charade • Days of Wine and Roses • Dear Heart • How Soon • Inspector Clouseau Theme • It Had Better Be Tonight • Moment to Moment • Moon River.
00118878 ....$14.99

Meaningful Moments
Eight memorable pieces: Adagio • Bridal March • Elegy • Recessional • Wedding March • Wedding Processional. Plus, arrangements of beloved favorites Amazing Grace and Ave Maria.
00279100 ....$9.99

New Orleans Sketches
Titles: Big Easy Blues • Bourbon Street Beat • Carnival Capers • Jivin' in Jackson Square • Masquerade! • Rex Parade.
00139675..$12.99

On the Jazzy Side
Six original solos. Songs: High Five! • Jubilation! • Prime Time • Small Talk • Small Town Blues • Travelin' Light.
00311982..$12.99

HAL•LEONARD®
www.halleonard.com

Prices, contents, and availability subject to change without notice and may vary outside the U.S.A.

Recuerdos Hispanicos
Seven original solos: Brisas Isleñas (Island Breezes) • Dia de Fiesta (Holiday) • Un Amor Quebrado (A Lost Love) • Resonancias de España (Echoes of Spain) • Niña Bonita (Pretty Girl) • Fantasia del Mambo (Mambo Fantasy) • Cuentos del Matador (Tales of the Matador).
00311369..$9.99

Rodgers & Hammerstein Selected Favorites
Eight favorites: Climb Ev'ry Mountain • Do-Re-Mi • If I Loved You • Oklahoma • Shall We Dance? • Some Enchanted Evening • There Is Nothin' like a Dame • You'll Never Walk Alone. Includes a CD of Eugénie performing each song.
00311928..$14.99

Romantic Stylings
Eight original piano solos: Cafe de Paris • Celebracion • Last Dance • Longings • Memento • Rapsodie • Reflections • Romance.
00312272 ....$14.99

Swingin' the Blues
Six blues originals: Back Street Blues • Big Shot Blues • Easy Walkin' Blues • Hometown Blues • Late Night Blues • Two-Way Blues.
00311445..$12.95

Two's Company
Titles: Island Holiday • La Danza • Mood in Blue • Postcript • Whimsical Waltz.
00311883 ....$12.99

Valses Sentimentales
Seven original solos: Bal Masque (Masked Ball) • Jardin de Thé (Tea Garden) • Le Long du Boulevard (Along the Boulevard) • Marché aux Fleurs (Flower Market) • Nuit sans Etoiles (Night Without Stars) • Palais Royale (Royal Palace) • Promenade á Deux (Strolling Together).
00311497..$9.99